50 Smoothie Recipes for Home

By: Kelly Johnson

Table of Contents

- Green Power Smoothie
- Berry Blast Smoothie
- Tropical Paradise Smoothie
- Chocolate Banana Smoothie
- Mango Tango Smoothie
- Kale and Pineapple Smoothie
- Blueberry Almond Smoothie
- Strawberry Spinach Smoothie
- Peanut Butter Banana Smoothie
- Avocado Mango Smoothie
- Raspberry Coconut Smoothie
- Orange Creamsicle Smoothie
- Pina Colada Smoothie
- Apple Cinnamon Smoothie
- Spinach Berry Smoothie
- Watermelon Mint Smoothie
- Carrot Ginger Smoothie
- Kiwi Strawberry Smoothie
- Oatmeal Cookie Smoothie
- Pineapple Kale Smoothie
- Cherry Vanilla Smoothie
- Lemon Blueberry Smoothie
- Almond Joy Smoothie
- Peach Raspberry Smoothie
- Banana Nut Smoothie
- Cucumber Mint Smoothie
- Chai Spice Smoothie
- Blackberry Basil Smoothie
- Honeydew Melon Smoothie
- Mango Lassi Smoothie
- Chocolate Raspberry Smoothie
- Peanut Butter Cup Smoothie
- Cranberry Orange Smoothie
- Green Tea Smoothie
- Strawberry Lime Smoothie
- Beetroot Berry Smoothie

- Cantaloupe Ginger Smoothie
- Vanilla Fig Smoothie
- Blueberry Avocado Smoothie
- Sweet Potato Pie Smoothie
- Coconut Watermelon Smoothie
- Espresso Banana Smoothie
- Chocolate Cherry Smoothie
- Apricot Almond Smoothie
- Turmeric Mango Smoothie
- Pistachio Date Smoothie
- Pear Ginger Smoothie
- Spiced Apple Smoothie
- Raspberry Beet Smoothie
- Pineapple Coconut Smoothie

Green Power Smoothie

Ingredients:

- 1 cup spinach (fresh or frozen)
- 1/2 cup kale (fresh or frozen)
- 1/2 cucumber, peeled and chopped
- 1/2 green apple, cored and chopped
- 1/2 avocado, peeled and pitted
- Juice of 1/2 lemon
- 1 tablespoon chia seeds
- 1 cup unsweetened almond milk or coconut water
- Optional: a few ice cubes for a colder smoothie

Instructions:

1. Add spinach, kale, cucumber, green apple, avocado, lemon juice, chia seeds, and almond milk (or coconut water) to a blender.
2. Blend on high until smooth and creamy.
3. If the smoothie is too thick, add more almond milk or coconut water until desired consistency is reached.
4. Pour into a glass and serve immediately.

This Green Power Smoothie is packed with vitamins, minerals, fiber, and healthy fats from the avocado and chia seeds. It's a great way to start your day or refuel after a workout!

Berry Blast Smoothie

Ingredients:

- 1 cup mixed berries (such as strawberries, blueberries, raspberries)
- 1/2 cup plain Greek yogurt
- 1/2 banana, frozen
- 1/2 cup spinach (optional, for added nutrition)
- 1 tablespoon honey or maple syrup (optional, for sweetness)
- 1/2 cup almond milk or any milk of your choice
- Ice cubes (optional, for a colder smoothie)

Instructions:

1. Add mixed berries, Greek yogurt, frozen banana, spinach (if using), honey or maple syrup (if using), and almond milk to a blender.
2. Blend on high until smooth and creamy.
3. If the smoothie is too thick, add more almond milk as needed until desired consistency is reached.
4. If you prefer a colder smoothie, add a few ice cubes and blend again until smooth.
5. Pour into a glass and enjoy your refreshing Berry Blast Smoothie!

This smoothie is rich in antioxidants from the berries, protein from the Greek yogurt, and potassium from the banana. It's perfect for breakfast, a snack, or even as a post-workout refresher!

Tropical Paradise Smoothie

Ingredients:

- 1 cup frozen mango chunks
- 1/2 cup frozen pineapple chunks
- 1/2 banana, frozen
- 1/2 cup coconut milk (or coconut water for a lighter option)
- 1/2 cup orange juice
- 1 tablespoon shredded coconut (optional, for extra tropical flavor)
- Ice cubes (optional, for a colder smoothie)

Instructions:

1. Add frozen mango chunks, frozen pineapple chunks, frozen banana, coconut milk (or coconut water), and orange juice to a blender.
2. Blend on high until smooth and creamy.
3. If the smoothie is too thick, add more coconut milk or orange juice as needed until desired consistency is reached.
4. If you want a colder smoothie, add a few ice cubes and blend again until smooth.
5. Optionally, sprinkle shredded coconut on top for garnish and extra tropical flavor.
6. Pour into a glass, garnish with shredded coconut if desired, and enjoy your Tropical Paradise Smoothie!

This smoothie is bursting with tropical fruit flavors and is rich in vitamins, minerals, and fiber. It's a perfect way to start your day with a taste of paradise!

Chocolate Banana Smoothie

Ingredients:

- 1 banana, preferably frozen
- 1 tablespoon cocoa powder (unsweetened)
- 1 tablespoon almond butter or peanut butter
- 1 cup milk of your choice (almond milk, soy milk, dairy milk)
- 1 tablespoon honey or maple syrup (optional, for added sweetness)
- Ice cubes (optional, for a colder smoothie)

Instructions:

1. Peel and slice the banana. If you prefer a colder smoothie, use a frozen banana.
2. Add the banana slices, cocoa powder, almond butter or peanut butter, milk of your choice, and honey or maple syrup (if using) to a blender.
3. Blend on high until smooth and creamy. If the smoothie is too thick, add more milk a little at a time until desired consistency is reached.
4. If you want a colder smoothie, add a few ice cubes and blend again until smooth.
5. Pour into a glass and serve immediately.

This Chocolate Banana Smoothie is rich in potassium from the banana, antioxidants from the cocoa powder, and healthy fats from the almond butter or peanut butter. It's a great treat for breakfast, a snack, or even a healthy dessert option!

Mango Tango Smoothie

Ingredients:

- 1 cup frozen mango chunks
- 1/2 cup plain Greek yogurt
- 1/2 banana, frozen
- 1/2 cup orange juice (freshly squeezed if possible)
- 1/4 cup coconut milk (optional, for a creamier texture)
- 1 tablespoon honey or maple syrup (optional, for added sweetness)
- Ice cubes (optional, for a colder smoothie)

Instructions:

1. Add frozen mango chunks, Greek yogurt, frozen banana, orange juice, coconut milk (if using), and honey or maple syrup (if using) to a blender.
2. Blend on high until smooth and creamy. If the smoothie is too thick, add more orange juice or coconut milk as needed until desired consistency is reached.
3. If you prefer a colder smoothie, add a few ice cubes and blend again until smooth.
4. Pour into a glass and serve immediately.

This Mango Tango Smoothie is packed with vitamin C from the mango and orange juice, protein from the Greek yogurt, and natural sweetness from the fruits. It's a tropical delight that's perfect for a sunny morning or a refreshing afternoon pick-me-up!

Kale and Pineapple Smoothie

Ingredients:

- 1 cup chopped kale leaves (stems removed)
- 1 cup frozen pineapple chunks
- 1/2 banana, frozen
- 1/2 cup plain Greek yogurt or coconut yogurt
- 1 tablespoon chia seeds or flax seeds
- 1 cup unsweetened almond milk or coconut water
- Optional: honey or maple syrup for added sweetness
- Ice cubes (optional, for a colder smoothie)

Instructions:

1. Place chopped kale leaves, frozen pineapple chunks, frozen banana, Greek yogurt or coconut yogurt, chia seeds or flax seeds, and almond milk or coconut water in a blender.
2. Blend on high speed until smooth and creamy. If the smoothie is too thick, add more almond milk or coconut water gradually until desired consistency is reached.
3. Taste and add honey or maple syrup if you prefer a sweeter smoothie.
4. For a colder smoothie, add a few ice cubes and blend again until smooth.

5. Pour into glasses and serve immediately.

This Kale and Pineapple Smoothie is packed with vitamins, minerals, and fiber from the kale and pineapple. It's refreshing, nutritious, and makes for a great breakfast or snack to start your day on a healthy note!

Blueberry Almond Smoothie

Ingredients:

- 1 cup frozen blueberries
- 1 banana, preferably frozen
- 1/4 cup rolled oats
- 1 tablespoon almond butter
- 1 cup almond milk (or any milk of your choice)
- 1 tablespoon honey or maple syrup (optional, for added sweetness)
- Ice cubes (optional, for a colder smoothie)

Instructions:

1. Place frozen blueberries, banana (if frozen), rolled oats, almond butter, almond milk, and honey or maple syrup (if using) into a blender.
2. Blend on high until smooth and creamy. If the smoothie is too thick, add more almond milk gradually until desired consistency is reached.
3. If you prefer a colder smoothie, add a few ice cubes and blend again until smooth.
4. Pour into glasses and serve immediately.

This Blueberry Almond Smoothie is packed with antioxidants from the blueberries, fiber and protein from the oats and almond butter, and it's naturally sweetened with banana and optional honey or maple syrup. It's a nutritious and satisfying smoothie that's perfect for breakfast or as a snack!

Strawberry Spinach Smoothie

Ingredients:

- 1 cup fresh or frozen strawberries
- 1 cup fresh spinach leaves
- 1/2 banana, frozen
- 1/2 cup plain Greek yogurt or coconut yogurt
- 1 tablespoon chia seeds or flax seeds (optional)
- 1 cup unsweetened almond milk or any milk of your choice
- Optional: honey or maple syrup for added sweetness
- Ice cubes (optional, for a colder smoothie)

Instructions:

1. Place strawberries, spinach leaves, frozen banana, Greek yogurt or coconut yogurt, chia seeds or flax seeds (if using), and almond milk into a blender.
2. Blend on high until smooth and creamy. If the smoothie is too thick, add more almond milk gradually until desired consistency is reached.
3. Taste and add honey or maple syrup if you prefer a sweeter smoothie.
4. For a colder smoothie, add a few ice cubes and blend again until smooth.
5. Pour into glasses and serve immediately.

This Strawberry Spinach Smoothie combines the sweetness of strawberries with the nutritional benefits of spinach, providing vitamins, minerals, and fiber. It's a refreshing and healthy option for breakfast or a snack!

Peanut Butter Banana Smoothie

Ingredients:

- 1 banana, preferably frozen
- 1 tablespoon peanut butter (natural, unsweetened)
- 1 tablespoon honey or maple syrup (optional, for added sweetness)
- 1 cup milk of your choice (almond milk, dairy milk, soy milk)
- 1/4 cup rolled oats (optional, for added fiber and texture)
- Ice cubes (optional, for a colder smoothie)

Instructions:

1. Peel and slice the banana. If you prefer a colder smoothie, use a frozen banana.
2. In a blender, combine the banana, peanut butter, honey or maple syrup (if using), milk, and rolled oats (if using).
3. Blend on high speed until smooth and creamy. If the smoothie is too thick, add more milk gradually until desired consistency is reached.
4. If you want a colder smoothie, add a few ice cubes and blend again until smooth.

5. Pour into a glass and serve immediately.

This Peanut Butter Banana Smoothie is rich in potassium from the banana, protein and healthy fats from the peanut butter, and can be customized with additional ingredients like oats for added fiber. It's a perfect breakfast option or a satisfying post-workout drink!

Avocado Mango Smoothie

Ingredients:

- 1/2 ripe avocado, peeled and pitted
- 1 cup frozen mango chunks
- 1/2 banana, frozen
- 1 tablespoon honey or maple syrup (optional, for added sweetness)
- 1 cup coconut water or almond milk
- Juice of 1/2 lime (optional, for a tangy twist)
- Ice cubes (optional, for a colder smoothie)

Instructions:

1. Scoop the flesh of the avocado into a blender.
2. Add frozen mango chunks, frozen banana, honey or maple syrup (if using), coconut water or almond milk, and lime juice (if using).
3. Blend on high speed until smooth and creamy. If the smoothie is too thick, add more coconut water or almond milk gradually until desired consistency is reached.
4. If you prefer a colder smoothie, add a few ice cubes and blend again until smooth.
5. Pour into glasses and serve immediately.

This Avocado Mango Smoothie is rich in healthy fats from the avocado, vitamins and fiber from the mango, and provides a creamy texture with a tropical flavor. It's perfect for breakfast or as a refreshing snack any time of the day!

Raspberry Coconut Smoothie

Ingredients:

- 1 cup frozen raspberries
- 1/2 cup coconut milk (from a can for a creamier texture)
- 1/2 cup plain Greek yogurt or coconut yogurt
- 1 tablespoon honey or maple syrup (optional, for added sweetness)
- 1/2 banana, frozen (optional, for added creaminess)
- 1 tablespoon chia seeds (optional, for extra nutrition)
- Ice cubes (optional, for a colder smoothie)

Instructions:

1. Place frozen raspberries, coconut milk, Greek yogurt or coconut yogurt, honey or maple syrup (if using), and banana (if using) into a blender.
2. Add chia seeds for added nutrition, if desired.
3. Blend on high speed until smooth and creamy. If the smoothie is too thick, add more coconut milk or a splash of water gradually until desired consistency is reached.
4. If you prefer a colder smoothie, add a few ice cubes and blend again until smooth.
5. Pour into glasses and serve immediately.

This Raspberry Coconut Smoothie is packed with antioxidants from the raspberries, healthy fats from the coconut milk, and probiotics from the Greek yogurt or coconut yogurt. It's a refreshing and nutritious smoothie option for any time of the day!

Orange Creamsicle Smoothie

Ingredients:

- 1 cup orange juice (freshly squeezed for best flavor)
- 1/2 cup plain Greek yogurt or vanilla yogurt
- 1/2 cup frozen mango chunks
- 1/2 banana, frozen
- 1 tablespoon honey or maple syrup (optional, for added sweetness)
- 1/2 teaspoon vanilla extract
- Ice cubes (optional, for a colder smoothie)

Instructions:

1. In a blender, combine orange juice, Greek yogurt or vanilla yogurt, frozen mango chunks, frozen banana, honey or maple syrup (if using), and vanilla extract.
2. Blend on high speed until smooth and creamy. If the smoothie is too thick, add more orange juice or a splash of water gradually until desired consistency is reached.
3. If you prefer a colder smoothie, add a few ice cubes and blend again until smooth.
4. Taste and adjust sweetness if necessary by adding more honey or maple syrup.
5. Pour into glasses and serve immediately.

This Orange Creamsicle Smoothie captures the refreshing citrus flavor of oranges with a creamy texture from Greek yogurt and a hint of sweetness. It's a perfect treat for breakfast or a snack, especially on a hot day!

Pina Colada Smoothie

Ingredients:

- 1 cup frozen pineapple chunks
- 1/2 cup coconut milk (from a can for a creamier texture)
- 1/2 cup plain Greek yogurt or coconut yogurt
- 1/2 banana, frozen (optional, for added creaminess)
- 1 tablespoon shredded coconut (optional, for extra coconut flavor)
- 1 tablespoon honey or maple syrup (optional, for added sweetness)
- 1/2 teaspoon vanilla extract
- Ice cubes (optional, for a colder smoothie)

Instructions:

1. In a blender, combine frozen pineapple chunks, coconut milk, Greek yogurt or coconut yogurt, frozen banana (if using), shredded coconut (if using), honey or maple syrup (if using), and vanilla extract.
2. Blend on high speed until smooth and creamy. If the smoothie is too thick, add more coconut milk or a splash of water gradually until desired consistency is reached.
3. If you prefer a colder smoothie, add a few ice cubes and blend again until smooth.
4. Taste and adjust sweetness if necessary by adding more honey or maple syrup.
5. Pour into glasses, garnish with a pineapple slice or shredded coconut if desired, and enjoy your tropical Pina Colada Smoothie!

This smoothie captures the classic flavors of a Pina Colada with pineapple and coconut, and it's perfect for a refreshing breakfast or a healthy treat any time of the day!

Apple Cinnamon Smoothie

Ingredients:

- 1 apple, cored and chopped (use a sweet variety like Fuji or Honeycrisp)
- 1/2 cup plain Greek yogurt or vanilla yogurt
- 1/2 cup almond milk or any milk of your choice
- 1/4 cup rolled oats
- 1 tablespoon honey or maple syrup (optional, for added sweetness)
- 1/2 teaspoon ground cinnamon
- 1/4 teaspoon ground nutmeg (optional, for extra warmth)
- Ice cubes (optional, for a colder smoothie)

Instructions:

1. Place chopped apple, Greek yogurt or vanilla yogurt, almond milk, rolled oats, honey or maple syrup (if using), ground cinnamon, and ground nutmeg (if using) into a blender.
2. Blend on high speed until smooth and creamy. If the smoothie is too thick, add more almond milk gradually until desired consistency is reached.
3. If you prefer a colder smoothie, add a few ice cubes and blend again until smooth.
4. Taste and adjust sweetness or spice levels if necessary.
5. Pour into glasses, sprinkle a pinch of cinnamon on top for garnish if desired, and enjoy your Apple Cinnamon Smoothie!

This smoothie combines the natural sweetness of apples with warming spices like cinnamon and nutmeg, making it a comforting and nutritious choice for breakfast or a snack. It's also a great way to enjoy the flavors of fall year-round!

Spinach Berry Smoothie

Ingredients:

- 1 cup fresh spinach leaves
- 1/2 cup frozen mixed berries (such as strawberries, blueberries, raspberries)
- 1/2 banana, frozen
- 1 tablespoon chia seeds or flax seeds
- 1/2 cup plain Greek yogurt or coconut yogurt
- 1 cup unsweetened almond milk or any milk of your choice
- Optional: honey or maple syrup for added sweetness
- Ice cubes (optional, for a colder smoothie)

Instructions:

1. Place fresh spinach leaves, frozen mixed berries, frozen banana, chia seeds or flax seeds, Greek yogurt or coconut yogurt, almond milk, and honey or maple syrup (if using) into a blender.
2. Blend on high speed until smooth and creamy. If the smoothie is too thick, add more almond milk gradually until desired consistency is reached.
3. If you prefer a colder smoothie, add a few ice cubes and blend again until smooth.
4. Taste and adjust sweetness if necessary by adding more honey or maple syrup.
5. Pour into glasses and serve immediately.

This Spinach Berry Smoothie is rich in antioxidants from the berries, packed with vitamins and minerals from the spinach, and provides protein and probiotics from the Greek yogurt or coconut yogurt. It's a refreshing and nutritious way to start your day or to enjoy as a healthy snack!

Watermelon Mint Smoothie

Ingredients:

- 2 cups seedless watermelon, chopped
- 1/2 cup plain Greek yogurt or coconut yogurt
- Juice of 1/2 lime
- 5-6 fresh mint leaves
- 1 tablespoon honey or maple syrup (optional, for added sweetness)
- Ice cubes (optional, for a colder smoothie)

Instructions:

1. Place chopped watermelon, Greek yogurt or coconut yogurt, lime juice, mint leaves, and honey or maple syrup (if using) into a blender.
2. Blend on high speed until smooth and creamy. If the smoothie is too thick, add a splash of water or coconut water gradually until desired consistency is reached.
3. If you prefer a colder smoothie, add a few ice cubes and blend again until smooth.
4. Taste and adjust sweetness or tartness by adding more honey, lime juice, or mint leaves as desired.
5. Pour into glasses, garnish with a mint sprig or a slice of lime if desired, and enjoy your refreshing Watermelon Mint Smoothie!

This smoothie is hydrating and light, with the cooling flavor of watermelon complemented by the fresh mint and tangy lime. It's a perfect way to cool down and enjoy the flavors of summer!

Carrot Ginger Smoothie

Ingredients:

- 1 cup carrots, chopped (about 2 medium carrots)
- 1/2 inch piece of fresh ginger, peeled and chopped (adjust to taste)
- 1/2 cup plain Greek yogurt or coconut yogurt
- 1/2 cup orange juice (freshly squeezed if possible)
- 1 tablespoon honey or maple syrup (optional, for added sweetness)
- 1/2 teaspoon ground turmeric (optional, for added health benefits)
- Ice cubes (optional, for a colder smoothie)

Instructions:

1. Place chopped carrots, fresh ginger, Greek yogurt or coconut yogurt, orange juice, honey or maple syrup (if using), and ground turmeric (if using) into a blender.
2. Blend on high speed until smooth and creamy. If the smoothie is too thick, add a splash of water or orange juice gradually until desired consistency is reached.
3. If you prefer a colder smoothie, add a few ice cubes and blend again until smooth.
4. Taste and adjust sweetness or ginger intensity as desired.
5. Pour into glasses, garnish with a slice of carrot or a sprinkle of ground turmeric if desired, and enjoy your Carrot Ginger Smoothie!

This smoothie combines the natural sweetness of carrots with the zesty kick of ginger, and the tanginess of orange juice. It's a great way to incorporate more vegetables into your diet while enjoying a delicious and refreshing beverage!

Kiwi Strawberry Smoothie

Ingredients:

- 2 kiwis, peeled and chopped
- 1 cup fresh or frozen strawberries
- 1/2 banana, frozen (optional, for added creaminess)
- 1/2 cup plain Greek yogurt or coconut yogurt
- 1 tablespoon honey or maple syrup (optional, for added sweetness)
- 1/2 cup unsweetened almond milk or any milk of your choice
- Ice cubes (optional, for a colder smoothie)

Instructions:

1. Place chopped kiwis, strawberries, frozen banana (if using), Greek yogurt or coconut yogurt, honey or maple syrup (if using), and almond milk into a blender.
2. Blend on high speed until smooth and creamy. If the smoothie is too thick, add more almond milk gradually until desired consistency is reached.
3. If you prefer a colder smoothie, add a few ice cubes and blend again until smooth.
4. Taste and adjust sweetness if necessary by adding more honey or maple syrup.
5. Pour into glasses and serve immediately.

This Kiwi Strawberry Smoothie is packed with vitamin C from the kiwis and strawberries, probiotics from the Greek yogurt or coconut yogurt, and it's naturally sweetened with fruit. It's a refreshing and nutritious way to start your day or enjoy as a snack!

Oatmeal Cookie Smoothie

Ingredients:

- 1/2 cup rolled oats
- 1 banana, frozen
- 1 tablespoon almond butter or peanut butter
- 1 tablespoon honey or maple syrup (optional, for added sweetness)
- 1/2 teaspoon ground cinnamon
- 1/4 teaspoon ground nutmeg
- 1 cup unsweetened almond milk or any milk of your choice
- Ice cubes (optional, for a colder smoothie)

Instructions:

1. In a blender, combine rolled oats, frozen banana, almond butter or peanut butter, honey or maple syrup (if using), ground cinnamon, ground nutmeg, and almond milk.
2. Blend on high speed until smooth and creamy. If the smoothie is too thick, add more almond milk gradually until desired consistency is reached.
3. If you prefer a colder smoothie, add a few ice cubes and blend again until smooth.
4. Taste and adjust sweetness or spice levels if necessary.
5. Pour into glasses, sprinkle a pinch of cinnamon on top for garnish if desired, and enjoy your Oatmeal Cookie Smoothie!

This smoothie provides fiber from the oats, potassium and natural sweetness from the banana, protein and healthy fats from the almond butter or peanut butter, and warming spices like cinnamon and nutmeg. It's a delicious and satisfying option for breakfast or a snack, especially for those who enjoy the flavors of oatmeal cookies!

Pineapple Kale Smoothie

Ingredients:

- 1 cup chopped fresh kale leaves (stems removed)
- 1 cup frozen pineapple chunks
- 1/2 banana, frozen
- 1/2 cup plain Greek yogurt or coconut yogurt
- 1 tablespoon chia seeds or flax seeds (optional, for added nutrition)
- 1 cup unsweetened almond milk or any milk of your choice
- Ice cubes (optional, for a colder smoothie)

Instructions:

1. Place chopped kale leaves, frozen pineapple chunks, frozen banana, Greek yogurt or coconut yogurt, chia seeds or flax seeds (if using), and almond milk into a blender.
2. Blend on high speed until smooth and creamy. If the smoothie is too thick, add more almond milk gradually until desired consistency is reached.
3. If you prefer a colder smoothie, add a few ice cubes and blend again until smooth.
4. Pour into glasses and serve immediately.

This Pineapple Kale Smoothie is rich in vitamins, minerals, and antioxidants from the kale and pineapple. The Greek yogurt or coconut yogurt adds creaminess and probiotics, while chia seeds or flax seeds contribute omega-3 fatty acids and fiber. It's a nutritious and delicious way to incorporate kale into your diet!

Cherry Vanilla Smoothie

Ingredients:

- 1 cup frozen cherries
- 1/2 cup plain Greek yogurt or vanilla yogurt
- 1/2 cup almond milk or any milk of your choice
- 1/2 teaspoon vanilla extract
- 1 tablespoon honey or maple syrup (optional, for added sweetness)
- Ice cubes (optional, for a colder smoothie)

Instructions:

1. Place frozen cherries, Greek yogurt or vanilla yogurt, almond milk, vanilla extract, and honey or maple syrup (if using) into a blender.
2. Blend on high speed until smooth and creamy. If the smoothie is too thick, add more almond milk gradually until desired consistency is reached.
3. If you prefer a colder smoothie, add a few ice cubes and blend again until smooth.
4. Taste and adjust sweetness if necessary by adding more honey or maple syrup.
5. Pour into glasses and serve immediately.

This Cherry Vanilla Smoothie is rich in antioxidants from the cherries, protein from the Greek yogurt, and has a delightful vanilla flavor. It's a perfect breakfast option or a refreshing snack any time of the day!

Lemon Blueberry Smoothie

Ingredients:

- 1 cup fresh or frozen blueberries
- Juice of 1/2 lemon
- 1/2 cup plain Greek yogurt or vanilla yogurt
- 1 tablespoon honey or maple syrup (optional, for added sweetness)
- 1/2 cup almond milk or any milk of your choice
- Ice cubes (optional, for a colder smoothie)

Instructions:

1. Place blueberries, lemon juice, Greek yogurt or vanilla yogurt, honey or maple syrup (if using), and almond milk into a blender.
2. Blend on high speed until smooth and creamy. If the smoothie is too thick, add more almond milk gradually until desired consistency is reached.
3. If you prefer a colder smoothie, add a few ice cubes and blend again until smooth.
4. Taste and adjust sweetness or tartness by adding more honey or lemon juice as desired.
5. Pour into glasses and serve immediately.

This Lemon Blueberry Smoothie is packed with antioxidants from the blueberries and vitamin C from the lemon juice. The Greek yogurt adds protein and creaminess, while the honey or maple syrup provides optional sweetness. It's a refreshing and nutritious smoothie that's perfect for breakfast or a healthy snack!

Almond Joy Smoothie

Ingredients:

- 1 banana, frozen
- 1/4 cup shredded coconut (unsweetened)
- 1 tablespoon cocoa powder (unsweetened)
- 1 tablespoon almond butter
- 1 cup almond milk (or any milk of your choice)
- 1 tablespoon honey or maple syrup (optional, for added sweetness)
- Ice cubes (optional, for a colder smoothie)

Instructions:

1. Place frozen banana, shredded coconut, cocoa powder, almond butter, almond milk, and honey or maple syrup (if using) into a blender.
2. Blend on high speed until smooth and creamy. If the smoothie is too thick, add more almond milk gradually until desired consistency is reached.
3. If you prefer a colder smoothie, add a few ice cubes and blend again until smooth.
4. Taste and adjust sweetness if necessary by adding more honey or maple syrup.
5. Pour into glasses, sprinkle some shredded coconut on top for garnish if desired, and enjoy your Almond Joy Smoothie!

This smoothie combines the rich flavors of chocolate and almond with the sweetness of banana and coconut. It's a nutritious and satisfying treat that can be enjoyed for breakfast, as a snack, or even as a healthier dessert option!

Peach Raspberry Smoothie

Ingredients:

- 1 cup frozen peach slices
- 1/2 cup fresh or frozen raspberries
- 1/2 banana, frozen
- 1/2 cup plain Greek yogurt or vanilla yogurt
- 1 tablespoon honey or maple syrup (optional, for added sweetness)
- 1/2 cup almond milk or any milk of your choice
- Ice cubes (optional, for a colder smoothie)

Instructions:

1. Place frozen peach slices, raspberries, frozen banana, Greek yogurt or vanilla yogurt, honey or maple syrup (if using), and almond milk into a blender.
2. Blend on high speed until smooth and creamy. If the smoothie is too thick, add more almond milk gradually until desired consistency is reached.
3. If you prefer a colder smoothie, add a few ice cubes and blend again until smooth.
4. Taste and adjust sweetness if necessary by adding more honey or maple syrup.
5. Pour into glasses and serve immediately.

This Peach Raspberry Smoothie is packed with vitamins, antioxidants, and probiotics from the yogurt. It's a refreshing and nutritious way to enjoy the flavors of summer in a drink!

Banana Nut Smoothie

Ingredients:

- 1 banana, preferably frozen
- 1/4 cup nuts (such as almonds, walnuts, or pecans), soaked overnight or briefly toasted for added flavor
- 1 tablespoon nut butter (almond butter, peanut butter, or any nut butter of your choice)
- 1 tablespoon honey or maple syrup (optional, for added sweetness)
- 1 cup milk of your choice (almond milk, dairy milk, soy milk)
- 1/4 teaspoon ground cinnamon (optional, for added flavor)
- Ice cubes (optional, for a colder smoothie)

Instructions:

1. If you haven't soaked the nuts overnight, you can briefly toast them in a dry pan over medium heat for a few minutes until fragrant.
2. Place the banana, soaked or toasted nuts, nut butter, honey or maple syrup (if using), milk, and ground cinnamon (if using) into a blender.
3. Blend on high speed until smooth and creamy. If the smoothie is too thick, add more milk gradually until desired consistency is reached.
4. If you prefer a colder smoothie, add a few ice cubes and blend again until smooth.
5. Taste and adjust sweetness if necessary by adding more honey or maple syrup.
6. Pour into glasses, garnish with a sprinkle of cinnamon or chopped nuts if desired, and enjoy your Banana Nut Smoothie!

This smoothie is packed with protein from the nuts and nut butter, potassium from the banana, and can be customized with your choice of milk and additional flavors like cinnamon for a delicious and nutritious breakfast or snack!

Cucumber Mint Smoothie

Ingredients:

- 1 cucumber, peeled and chopped
- Handful of fresh mint leaves
- Juice of 1 lime
- 1/2 cup plain Greek yogurt or coconut yogurt
- 1 tablespoon honey or maple syrup (optional, for added sweetness)
- 1 cup coconut water or water
- Ice cubes (optional, for a colder smoothie)

Instructions:

1. Place chopped cucumber, fresh mint leaves, lime juice, Greek yogurt or coconut yogurt, honey or maple syrup (if using), and coconut water or water into a blender.
2. Blend on high speed until smooth and creamy. If the smoothie is too thick, add more coconut water or water gradually until desired consistency is reached.
3. If you prefer a colder smoothie, add a few ice cubes and blend again until smooth.
4. Taste and adjust sweetness or tartness by adding more honey or lime juice as desired.
5. Pour into glasses, garnish with a mint leaf if desired, and enjoy your refreshing Cucumber Mint Smoothie!

This smoothie is hydrating from the cucumber and coconut water, and the mint adds a refreshing and cooling flavor. It's perfect for a hot day or as a light and healthy breakfast option!

Chai Spice Smoothie

Ingredients:

- 1 cup unsweetened almond milk or any milk of your choice
- 1/2 cup plain Greek yogurt or vanilla yogurt
- 1 banana, frozen
- 1/2 teaspoon ground cinnamon
- 1/4 teaspoon ground ginger
- 1/4 teaspoon ground cardamom
- 1/8 teaspoon ground cloves
- 1/8 teaspoon ground nutmeg
- 1 tablespoon honey or maple syrup (optional, for added sweetness)
- Ice cubes (optional, for a colder smoothie)

Instructions:

1. In a blender, combine almond milk, Greek yogurt, frozen banana, ground cinnamon, ground ginger, ground cardamom, ground cloves, ground nutmeg, and honey or maple syrup (if using).
2. Blend on high speed until smooth and creamy. If the smoothie is too thick, add more almond milk gradually until desired consistency is reached.
3. If you prefer a colder smoothie, add a few ice cubes and blend again until smooth.
4. Taste and adjust sweetness or spice levels if necessary.
5. Pour into glasses, sprinkle a pinch of cinnamon on top for garnish if desired, and enjoy your Chai Spice Smoothie!

This smoothie captures the comforting and aromatic flavors of chai tea in a nutritious beverage. It's a perfect way to start your day or to enjoy as a flavorful snack!

Blackberry Basil Smoothie

Ingredients:

- 1 cup fresh or frozen blackberries
- Handful of fresh basil leaves
- 1/2 cup plain Greek yogurt or coconut yogurt
- 1 tablespoon honey or maple syrup (optional, for added sweetness)
- 1/2 cup almond milk or any milk of your choice
- Juice of 1/2 lime (optional, for a tangy twist)
- Ice cubes (optional, for a colder smoothie)

Instructions:

1. Place blackberries, fresh basil leaves, Greek yogurt or coconut yogurt, honey or maple syrup (if using), almond milk, and lime juice (if using) into a blender.
2. Blend on high speed until smooth and creamy. If the smoothie is too thick, add more almond milk gradually until desired consistency is reached.
3. If you prefer a colder smoothie, add a few ice cubes and blend again until smooth.
4. Taste and adjust sweetness or tartness by adding more honey, lime juice, or basil leaves as desired.
5. Pour into glasses, garnish with a basil leaf or a few blackberries if desired, and enjoy your refreshing Blackberry Basil Smoothie!

This smoothie is packed with antioxidants from the blackberries, vitamins and minerals from the basil, and probiotics from the Greek yogurt or coconut yogurt. It's a delightful and nutritious way to enjoy the flavors of summer!

Honeydew Melon Smoothie

Ingredients:

- 2 cups diced honeydew melon (fresh or frozen)
- 1/2 cup plain Greek yogurt or coconut yogurt
- 1 tablespoon honey or maple syrup (optional, for added sweetness)
- Juice of 1/2 lime (optional, for a tangy twist)
- 1/2 cup coconut water or water
- Ice cubes (optional, for a colder smoothie)

Instructions:

1. Place diced honeydew melon, Greek yogurt or coconut yogurt, honey or maple syrup (if using), lime juice (if using), and coconut water or water into a blender.
2. Blend on high speed until smooth and creamy. If the smoothie is too thick, add more coconut water or water gradually until desired consistency is reached.
3. If you prefer a colder smoothie, add a few ice cubes and blend again until smooth.
4. Taste and adjust sweetness or tartness by adding more honey or lime juice as desired.
5. Pour into glasses, garnish with a slice of honeydew melon or a wedge of lime if desired, and enjoy your refreshing Honeydew Melon Smoothie!

This smoothie highlights the sweet and juicy flavor of honeydew melon, complemented by the creamy texture of Greek yogurt or coconut yogurt. It's a hydrating and nutritious beverage that's perfect for breakfast or a refreshing snack!

Mango Lassi Smoothie

Ingredients:

- 1 cup diced ripe mango (fresh or frozen)
- 1/2 cup plain Greek yogurt or coconut yogurt
- 1/2 cup milk (dairy or plant-based)
- 1 tablespoon honey or maple syrup (optional, for added sweetness)
- 1/4 teaspoon ground cardamom (optional, for authentic flavor)
- Ice cubes (optional, for a colder smoothie)

Instructions:

1. Place diced mango, Greek yogurt or coconut yogurt, milk, honey or maple syrup (if using), and ground cardamom (if using) into a blender.
2. Blend on high speed until smooth and creamy. If the smoothie is too thick, add a little more milk gradually until desired consistency is reached.
3. If you prefer a colder smoothie, add a few ice cubes and blend again until smooth.
4. Taste and adjust sweetness or cardamom flavor if necessary.
5. Pour into glasses, garnish with a sprinkle of ground cardamom or a slice of mango if desired, and enjoy your Mango Lassi Smoothie!

This Mango Lassi Smoothie captures the tropical sweetness of mangoes with the tanginess of yogurt, creating a refreshing and nutritious drink. It's perfect for cooling down on a warm day or enjoying as a creamy treat!

Chocolate Raspberry Smoothie

Ingredients:

- 1 cup frozen raspberries
- 1 tablespoon cocoa powder (unsweetened)
- 1/2 cup plain Greek yogurt or vanilla yogurt
- 1 tablespoon honey or maple syrup (optional, for added sweetness)
- 1 cup almond milk or any milk of your choice
- Ice cubes (optional, for a colder smoothie)

Instructions:

1. Place frozen raspberries, cocoa powder, Greek yogurt or vanilla yogurt, honey or maple syrup (if using), and almond milk into a blender.
2. Blend on high speed until smooth and creamy. If the smoothie is too thick, add more almond milk gradually until desired consistency is reached.
3. If you prefer a colder smoothie, add a few ice cubes and blend again until smooth.
4. Taste and adjust sweetness if necessary by adding more honey or maple syrup.
5. Pour into glasses, garnish with a few raspberries or a sprinkle of cocoa powder if desired, and enjoy your Chocolate Raspberry Smoothie!

This smoothie is packed with antioxidants from the raspberries and cocoa powder, protein from the Greek yogurt, and is naturally sweetened with honey or maple syrup. It's a delicious and nutritious way to indulge in the flavors of chocolate and raspberries!

Peanut Butter Cup Smoothie

Ingredients:

- 1 banana, frozen
- 1 tablespoon cocoa powder (unsweetened)
- 1 tablespoon peanut butter (natural or unsweetened)
- 1 tablespoon honey or maple syrup (optional, for added sweetness)
- 1/2 cup plain Greek yogurt or vanilla yogurt
- 1 cup almond milk or any milk of your choice
- Ice cubes (optional, for a colder smoothie)

Instructions:

1. In a blender, combine frozen banana, cocoa powder, peanut butter, honey or maple syrup (if using), Greek yogurt or vanilla yogurt, and almond milk.
2. Blend on high speed until smooth and creamy. If the smoothie is too thick, add more almond milk gradually until desired consistency is reached.
3. If you prefer a colder smoothie, add a few ice cubes and blend again until smooth.
4. Taste and adjust sweetness if necessary by adding more honey or maple syrup.
5. Pour into glasses, garnish with a sprinkle of cocoa powder or a drizzle of peanut butter if desired, and enjoy your Peanut Butter Cup Smoothie!

This smoothie is rich in protein from the Greek yogurt and peanut butter, and provides a decadent chocolate flavor from the cocoa powder. It's a great option for a quick breakfast or a satisfying snack!

Cranberry Orange Smoothie

Ingredients:

- 1 cup fresh or frozen cranberries
- Juice and zest of 1 orange
- 1 banana, frozen
- 1/2 cup plain Greek yogurt or vanilla yogurt
- 1 tablespoon honey or maple syrup (optional, for added sweetness)
- 1/2 cup almond milk or any milk of your choice
- Ice cubes (optional, for a colder smoothie)

Instructions:

1. Place cranberries, orange juice and zest, frozen banana, Greek yogurt or vanilla yogurt, honey or maple syrup (if using), and almond milk into a blender.
2. Blend on high speed until smooth and creamy. If the smoothie is too thick, add more almond milk gradually until desired consistency is reached.
3. If you prefer a colder smoothie, add a few ice cubes and blend again until smooth.
4. Taste and adjust sweetness or tartness by adding more honey or orange juice as desired.
5. Pour into glasses, garnish with a slice of orange or a few cranberries if desired, and enjoy your Cranberry Orange Smoothie!

This smoothie is a delightful blend of tart cranberries and citrusy orange, balanced with the creaminess of Greek yogurt and sweetness from honey or maple syrup. It's perfect for boosting your immune system and refreshing your palate!

Green Tea Smoothie

Ingredients:

- 1 cup brewed green tea, chilled
- 1 banana, frozen
- 1 cup spinach leaves (fresh or frozen)
- 1/2 cup pineapple chunks (fresh or frozen)
- Juice of 1/2 lemon
- 1 tablespoon honey or maple syrup (optional, for added sweetness)
- Ice cubes (optional, for a colder smoothie)

Instructions:

1. Brew green tea and let it cool to room temperature, then chill in the refrigerator until cold.
2. In a blender, combine chilled green tea, frozen banana, spinach leaves, pineapple chunks, lemon juice, and honey or maple syrup (if using).
3. Blend on high speed until smooth and creamy. If the smoothie is too thick, add a little water or more green tea gradually until desired consistency is reached.
4. If you prefer a colder smoothie, add a few ice cubes and blend again until smooth.
5. Taste and adjust sweetness or tartness by adding more honey or lemon juice as desired.
6. Pour into glasses, garnish with a slice of lemon or a sprig of mint if desired, and enjoy your Green Tea Smoothie!

This smoothie is rich in antioxidants from the green tea, vitamins and minerals from the spinach and pineapple, and provides a refreshing boost of energy. It's a great way to start your day or to enjoy as a pick-me-up in the afternoon!

Strawberry Lime Smoothie

Ingredients:

- 1 cup fresh or frozen strawberries
- Juice and zest of 1 lime
- 1/2 cup plain Greek yogurt or vanilla yogurt
- 1 tablespoon honey or maple syrup (optional, for added sweetness)
- 1/2 cup almond milk or any milk of your choice
- Ice cubes (optional, for a colder smoothie)

Instructions:

1. Place strawberries, lime juice and zest, Greek yogurt or vanilla yogurt, honey or maple syrup (if using), and almond milk into a blender.
2. Blend on high speed until smooth and creamy. If the smoothie is too thick, add more almond milk gradually until desired consistency is reached.
3. If you prefer a colder smoothie, add a few ice cubes and blend again until smooth.
4. Taste and adjust sweetness or tartness by adding more honey or lime juice as desired.
5. Pour into glasses, garnish with a slice of lime or a strawberry if desired, and enjoy your Strawberry Lime Smoothie!

This smoothie is packed with vitamin C from the strawberries and lime, protein from the Greek yogurt, and provides a delightful blend of sweet and tangy flavors. It's perfect for a refreshing breakfast or a healthy snack any time of the day!

Beetroot Berry Smoothie
IIngredients:

- 1 small beetroot, cooked and chopped (or use pre-cooked or canned)
- 1/2 cup mixed berries (such as strawberries, blueberries, raspberries)
- 1/2 banana, frozen
- 1/2 cup plain Greek yogurt or coconut yogurt
- 1 tablespoon honey or maple syrup (optional, for added sweetness)
- 1 cup almond milk or any milk of your choice
- Ice cubes (optional, for a colder smoothie)

Instructions:

1. If using fresh beetroot, cook it until tender, then peel and chop it. If using pre-cooked or canned beetroot, drain and chop it.
2. In a blender, combine the chopped beetroot, mixed berries, frozen banana, Greek yogurt or coconut yogurt, honey or maple syrup (if using), and almond milk.
3. Blend on high speed until smooth and creamy. If the smoothie is too thick, add more almond milk gradually until desired consistency is reached.
4. If you prefer a colder smoothie, add a few ice cubes and blend again until smooth.
5. Taste and adjust sweetness if necessary by adding more honey or maple syrup.
6. Pour into glasses, garnish with a few berries or a sprinkle of chia seeds if desired, and enjoy your Beetroot Berry Smoothie!

This smoothie is rich in antioxidants from the berries and beetroot, provides fiber and vitamins from the fruits and vegetables, and is creamy and satisfying thanks to the Greek yogurt or coconut yogurt. It's a nutritious and delicious way to incorporate beetroot into your diet!

Cantaloupe Ginger Smoothie

Ingredients:

- 2 cups diced cantaloupe
- 1 tablespoon fresh ginger, grated (adjust to taste)
- Juice of 1/2 lime
- 1/2 cup plain Greek yogurt or coconut yogurt
- 1 tablespoon honey or maple syrup (optional, for added sweetness)
- 1/2 cup almond milk or any milk of your choice
- Ice cubes (optional, for a colder smoothie)

Instructions:

1. Place diced cantaloupe, grated ginger, lime juice, Greek yogurt or coconut yogurt, honey or maple syrup (if using), and almond milk into a blender.
2. Blend on high speed until smooth and creamy. If the smoothie is too thick, add more almond milk gradually until desired consistency is reached.
3. If you prefer a colder smoothie, add a few ice cubes and blend again until smooth.
4. Taste and adjust sweetness or ginger intensity by adding more honey, lime juice, or ginger as desired.
5. Pour into glasses, garnish with a slice of cantaloupe or a sprinkle of grated ginger if desired, and enjoy your Cantaloupe Ginger Smoothie!

This smoothie combines the sweet and refreshing flavor of cantaloupe with the zingy kick of fresh ginger and the tanginess of lime. It's packed with vitamins, antioxidants, and probiotics from the yogurt, making it a healthy and invigorating choice for breakfast or a snack!

Vanilla Fig Smoothie

Ingredients:

- 2 ripe figs, stems removed and quartered
- 1 banana, frozen
- 1/2 cup plain Greek yogurt or vanilla yogurt
- 1/2 teaspoon vanilla extract
- 1 tablespoon honey or maple syrup (optional, for added sweetness)
- 1 cup almond milk or any milk of your choice
- Ice cubes (optional, for a colder smoothie)

Instructions:

1. Place quartered figs, frozen banana, Greek yogurt or vanilla yogurt, vanilla extract, honey or maple syrup (if using), and almond milk into a blender.
2. Blend on high speed until smooth and creamy. If the smoothie is too thick, add more almond milk gradually until desired consistency is reached.
3. If you prefer a colder smoothie, add a few ice cubes and blend again until smooth.
4. Taste and adjust sweetness if necessary by adding more honey or maple syrup.
5. Pour into glasses, garnish with a slice of fig or a sprinkle of vanilla extract if desired, and enjoy your Vanilla Fig Smoothie!

This smoothie combines the natural sweetness of figs with the creamy texture of yogurt and the aromatic flavor of vanilla. It's a delightful and nutritious way to enjoy the unique taste of figs in a refreshing drink!

Blueberry Avocado Smoothie

Ingredients:

- 1/2 ripe avocado
- 1 cup fresh or frozen blueberries
- 1 banana, frozen
- 1/2 cup spinach leaves (optional, for added nutrients)
- 1 tablespoon honey or maple syrup (optional, for added sweetness)
- 1 cup almond milk or any milk of your choice
- Ice cubes (optional, for a colder smoothie)

Instructions:

1. Scoop out the flesh of the avocado and place it in a blender.
2. Add blueberries, frozen banana, spinach leaves (if using), honey or maple syrup (if using), and almond milk into the blender.
3. Blend on high speed until smooth and creamy. If the smoothie is too thick, add more almond milk gradually until desired consistency is reached.
4. If you prefer a colder smoothie, add a few ice cubes and blend again until smooth.
5. Taste and adjust sweetness if necessary by adding more honey or maple syrup.
6. Pour into glasses, garnish with a few blueberries or a slice of avocado if desired, and enjoy your Blueberry Avocado Smoothie!

This smoothie is packed with healthy fats from the avocado, antioxidants from the blueberries, and potassium from the banana. It's a refreshing and satisfying drink that's perfect for breakfast or as a post-workout refuel!

Sweet Potato Pie Smoothie

Ingredients:

- 1 small sweet potato, cooked and peeled (about 1/2 cup mashed)
- 1/2 banana, frozen
- 1/2 cup plain Greek yogurt or vanilla yogurt
- 1/2 cup almond milk or any milk of your choice
- 1 tablespoon honey or maple syrup (optional, for added sweetness)
- 1/2 teaspoon ground cinnamon
- 1/4 teaspoon ground nutmeg
- 1/4 teaspoon ground ginger
- 1/4 teaspoon vanilla extract
- Ice cubes (optional, for a colder smoothie)

Instructions:

1. Cook the sweet potato until tender (you can bake, steam, or microwave it). Let it cool slightly, then peel and mash it.
2. In a blender, combine the mashed sweet potato, frozen banana, Greek yogurt or vanilla yogurt, almond milk, honey or maple syrup (if using), ground cinnamon, ground nutmeg, ground ginger, and vanilla extract.
3. Blend on high speed until smooth and creamy. If the smoothie is too thick, add more almond milk gradually until desired consistency is reached.
4. If you prefer a colder smoothie, add a few ice cubes and blend again until smooth.
5. Taste and adjust sweetness or spice levels if necessary.
6. Pour into glasses, sprinkle a little extra cinnamon on top for garnish if desired, and enjoy your Sweet Potato Pie Smoothie!

This smoothie captures the warm and comforting flavors of sweet potato pie, making it a nutritious and satisfying treat that's perfect for any time of day!

Coconut Watermelon Smoothie

Ingredients:

- 2 cups diced seedless watermelon
- 1/2 cup coconut water
- Juice of 1/2 lime
- 1 tablespoon honey or maple syrup (optional, for added sweetness)
- Ice cubes (optional, for a colder smoothie)

Instructions:

1. Place diced watermelon, coconut water, lime juice, and honey or maple syrup (if using) into a blender.
2. Blend on high speed until smooth and well combined.
3. If you prefer a colder smoothie, add a few ice cubes and blend again until smooth.
4. Taste and adjust sweetness or tartness by adding more honey or lime juice as desired.
5. Pour into glasses, garnish with a slice of lime or a small piece of watermelon if desired, and enjoy your refreshing Coconut Watermelon Smoothie!

This smoothie is hydrating from the coconut water and refreshing from the juicy watermelon. It's a perfect choice for a hot day or as a light and nutritious snack!

Espresso Banana Smoothie

Ingredients:

- 1 banana, frozen
- 1 shot of espresso (about 1-2 ounces), cooled
- 1/2 cup plain Greek yogurt or vanilla yogurt
- 1 tablespoon cocoa powder (optional, for added chocolate flavor)
- 1 tablespoon honey or maple syrup (optional, for added sweetness)
- 1/2 cup almond milk or any milk of your choice
- Ice cubes (optional, for a colder smoothie)

Instructions:

1. Brew a shot of espresso and let it cool to room temperature.
2. In a blender, combine the frozen banana, cooled espresso, Greek yogurt or vanilla yogurt, cocoa powder (if using), honey or maple syrup (if using), and almond milk.
3. Blend on high speed until smooth and creamy. If the smoothie is too thick, add more almond milk gradually until desired consistency is reached.
4. If you prefer a colder smoothie, add a few ice cubes and blend again until smooth.
5. Taste and adjust sweetness or coffee intensity by adding more honey or espresso as desired.
6. Pour into glasses, garnish with a sprinkle of cocoa powder or a few banana slices if desired, and enjoy your Espresso Banana Smoothie!

This smoothie provides a boost of energy from the espresso and potassium from the banana, making it a perfect pick-me-up for mornings or an afternoon treat!

Chocolate Cherry Smoothie

Ingredients:

- 1 cup frozen cherries
- 1 tablespoon cocoa powder (unsweetened)
- 1/2 cup plain Greek yogurt or vanilla yogurt
- 1 tablespoon honey or maple syrup (optional, for added sweetness)
- 1 cup almond milk or any milk of your choice
- Ice cubes (optional, for a colder smoothie)

Instructions:

1. Place frozen cherries, cocoa powder, Greek yogurt or vanilla yogurt, honey or maple syrup (if using), and almond milk into a blender.
2. Blend on high speed until smooth and creamy. If the smoothie is too thick, add more almond milk gradually until desired consistency is reached.
3. If you prefer a colder smoothie, add a few ice cubes and blend again until smooth.
4. Taste and adjust sweetness or chocolate intensity by adding more honey or cocoa powder as desired.
5. Pour into glasses, garnish with a few cherries or a sprinkle of cocoa powder if desired, and enjoy your Chocolate Cherry Smoothie!

This smoothie is rich in antioxidants from the cherries and cocoa powder, protein from the Greek yogurt, and provides a decadent chocolate flavor. It's a satisfying and nutritious treat that's perfect for satisfying chocolate cravings!

Apricot Almond Smoothie

Ingredients:

- 1 cup fresh or canned apricots (pitted and sliced), or use frozen apricots
- 1/4 cup raw almonds (soaked overnight or for a few hours, then drained)
- 1 banana, frozen
- 1/2 cup plain Greek yogurt or almond yogurt
- 1 tablespoon honey or maple syrup (optional, for added sweetness)
- 1 cup almond milk or any milk of your choice
- Ice cubes (optional, for a colder smoothie)

Instructions:

1. If using fresh apricots, make sure they are pitted and sliced. If using canned apricots, drain the syrup.
2. In a blender, combine the apricots, soaked almonds, frozen banana, Greek yogurt or almond yogurt, honey or maple syrup (if using), and almond milk.
3. Blend on high speed until smooth and creamy. If the smoothie is too thick, add more almond milk gradually until desired consistency is reached.
4. If you prefer a colder smoothie, add a few ice cubes and blend again until smooth.
5. Taste and adjust sweetness if necessary by adding more honey or maple syrup.
6. Pour into glasses, garnish with a slice of apricot or a sprinkle of chopped almonds if desired, and enjoy your Apricot Almond Smoothie!

This smoothie is packed with vitamins and minerals from the apricots and almonds, protein from the Greek yogurt, and healthy fats from the almonds. It's a delightful and nutritious way to start your day or to enjoy as a satisfying snack!

Turmeric Mango Smoothie

Ingredients:

- 1 cup diced mango (fresh or frozen)
- 1/2 teaspoon ground turmeric
- 1/2 teaspoon ground ginger (or 1 teaspoon grated fresh ginger)
- 1/2 cup plain Greek yogurt or coconut yogurt
- 1 tablespoon honey or maple syrup (optional, for added sweetness)
- 1 cup almond milk or any milk of your choice
- Ice cubes (optional, for a colder smoothie)

Instructions:

1. Place diced mango, ground turmeric, ground ginger or fresh grated ginger, Greek yogurt or coconut yogurt, honey or maple syrup (if using), and almond milk into a blender.
2. Blend on high speed until smooth and creamy. If the smoothie is too thick, add more almond milk gradually until desired consistency is reached.
3. If you prefer a colder smoothie, add a few ice cubes and blend again until smooth.
4. Taste and adjust sweetness or ginger/turmeric intensity by adding more honey, ginger, or turmeric as desired.
5. Pour into glasses, garnish with a sprinkle of ground turmeric or a slice of mango if desired, and enjoy your Turmeric Mango Smoothie!

This smoothie is packed with antioxidants and anti-inflammatory properties from turmeric and ginger, and provides a tropical burst of flavor from the mango. It's a refreshing and health-boosting drink that's perfect for any time of day!

Pistachio Date Smoothie

Ingredients:

- 1/4 cup shelled pistachios
- 6-8 pitted dates, soaked in hot water for 10 minutes if they are not soft
- 1 banana, frozen
- 1 cup plain Greek yogurt or almond yogurt
- 1 tablespoon honey or maple syrup (optional, for added sweetness)
- 1 cup almond milk or any milk of your choice
- Ice cubes (optional, for a colder smoothie)

Instructions:

1. If the dates are not soft, soak them in hot water for 10 minutes, then drain.
2. In a blender, combine the shelled pistachios, soaked dates, frozen banana, Greek yogurt or almond yogurt, honey or maple syrup (if using), and almond milk.
3. Blend on high speed until smooth and creamy. If the smoothie is too thick, add more almond milk gradually until desired consistency is reached.
4. If you prefer a colder smoothie, add a few ice cubes and blend again until smooth.
5. Taste and adjust sweetness if necessary by adding more honey or maple syrup.
6. Pour into glasses, garnish with a sprinkle of crushed pistachios if desired, and enjoy your Pistachio Date Smoothie!

This smoothie is rich in fiber and healthy fats from the pistachios and dates, provides protein from the Greek yogurt, and is naturally sweetened with dates. It's a satisfying and nutritious drink that's perfect for breakfast or as a post-workout refuel!

Pear Ginger Smoothie

Ingredients:

- 1 ripe pear, cored and chopped
- 1 teaspoon fresh ginger, grated (adjust to taste)
- 1/2 cup plain Greek yogurt or vanilla yogurt
- 1 tablespoon honey or maple syrup (optional, for added sweetness)
- 1 cup almond milk or any milk of your choice
- Ice cubes (optional, for a colder smoothie)

Instructions:

1. Place chopped pear, grated ginger, Greek yogurt or vanilla yogurt, honey or maple syrup (if using), and almond milk into a blender.
2. Blend on high speed until smooth and creamy. If the smoothie is too thick, add more almond milk gradually until desired consistency is reached.
3. If you prefer a colder smoothie, add a few ice cubes and blend again until smooth.
4. Taste and adjust sweetness or ginger intensity by adding more honey or ginger as desired.
5. Pour into glasses, garnish with a slice of pear or a sprinkle of grated ginger if desired, and enjoy your Pear Ginger Smoothie!

This smoothie is rich in fiber from the pear, provides a refreshing zing from the ginger, and is creamy thanks to the Greek yogurt. It's a perfect blend of flavors for a nutritious breakfast or a refreshing snack!

Spiced Apple Smoothie

Ingredients:

- 1 apple, cored and chopped (use sweet varieties like Gala or Fuji)
- 1/2 teaspoon ground cinnamon
- 1/4 teaspoon ground nutmeg
- 1/4 teaspoon ground cloves
- 1/2 cup plain Greek yogurt or vanilla yogurt
- 1 tablespoon honey or maple syrup (optional, for added sweetness)
- 1 cup almond milk or any milk of your choice
- Ice cubes (optional, for a colder smoothie)

Instructions:

1. Place chopped apple, ground cinnamon, ground nutmeg, ground cloves, Greek yogurt or vanilla yogurt, honey or maple syrup (if using), and almond milk into a blender.
2. Blend on high speed until smooth and creamy. If the smoothie is too thick, add more almond milk gradually until desired consistency is reached.
3. If you prefer a colder smoothie, add a few ice cubes and blend again until smooth.
4. Taste and adjust sweetness or spice levels by adding more honey, cinnamon, nutmeg, or cloves as desired.
5. Pour into glasses, sprinkle with a little extra cinnamon on top for garnish if desired, and enjoy your Spiced Apple Smoothie!

This smoothie captures the warm and comforting flavors of spiced apples, making it a perfect choice for a cozy fall morning or a nutritious snack any time of the day!

Raspberry Beet Smoothie

Ingredients:

- 1 cup fresh or frozen raspberries
- 1 small beetroot, cooked and peeled (about 1/2 cup chopped)
- 1/2 cup plain Greek yogurt or coconut yogurt
- 1 tablespoon honey or maple syrup (optional, for added sweetness)
- 1 cup almond milk or any milk of your choice
- Ice cubes (optional, for a colder smoothie)

Instructions:

1. Cook the beetroot until tender (you can bake, steam, or microwave it), then peel and chop.
2. In a blender, combine the raspberries, cooked and chopped beetroot, Greek yogurt or coconut yogurt, honey or maple syrup (if using), and almond milk.
3. Blend on high speed until smooth and creamy. If the smoothie is too thick, add more almond milk gradually until desired consistency is reached.
4. If you prefer a colder smoothie, add a few ice cubes and blend again until smooth.
5. Taste and adjust sweetness if necessary by adding more honey or maple syrup.
6. Pour into glasses, garnish with a few raspberries or a slice of beetroot if desired, and enjoy your Raspberry Beet Smoothie!

This smoothie is packed with antioxidants from the raspberries and beetroots, provides probiotics from the yogurt, and is a refreshing and nutritious way to incorporate beetroots into your diet!

Pineapple Coconut Smoothie

Ingredients:

- 1 cup fresh or frozen pineapple chunks
- 1/2 cup coconut milk
- 1/2 cup plain Greek yogurt or coconut yogurt
- 1 tablespoon honey or maple syrup (optional, for added sweetness)
- Juice of 1/2 lime (optional, for extra tang)
- Ice cubes (optional, for a colder smoothie)

Instructions:

1. In a blender, combine the pineapple chunks, coconut milk, Greek yogurt or coconut yogurt, honey or maple syrup (if using), and lime juice (if using).
2. Blend on high speed until smooth and creamy. If the smoothie is too thick, add more coconut milk gradually until desired consistency is reached.
3. If you prefer a colder smoothie, add a few ice cubes and blend again until smooth.
4. Taste and adjust sweetness or tanginess by adding more honey, maple syrup, or lime juice as desired.
5. Pour into glasses, garnish with a slice of pineapple or a sprinkle of shredded coconut if desired, and enjoy your Pineapple Coconut Smoothie!

This smoothie is rich in tropical flavors from the pineapple and coconut, creamy from the yogurt, and provides a refreshing taste of the islands. It's perfect for breakfast, a snack, or a refreshing drink on a hot day!